IMAGES OF ENGLAND

Around Coleshill

Grandpa Ensor, Deep Lane, Nether Whitacre, c. 1890. (W.G. Chambers) William Ryton Ensor was a typical Warwickshire farm labourer, working latterly at Croxall Farm for the Oldhams. He and his wife had few kitchen facilities in their tiny cottage; instead they did most of their cooking on an open fire at the rear of the property. Laced boots, corduroy trousers with leather ties below the knee, corduroy waistcoat, fustian coat, knotted neck-tie and felt hat made up his working attire.

IMAGES OF ENGLAND

Around Coleshill

John Bland & Colin Hayfield

NONSUCH

Cottager, Coleshill area, *c.* 1905. (F.D. Spencer)

First published 1996
This new pocket edition 2006
Images unchanged from first edition

Nonsuch Publishing Limited
The Mill, Brimscombe Port,
Stroud, Gloucestershire, GL5 2QG
www.nonsuch-publishing.com

Nonsuch Publishing is an imprint of Tempus Publishing Group

British Library Cataloguing in Publication Data.
A catalogue record for this book is available from the British Library.

ISBN 1-84588-265-2

Typesetting and origination by Nonsuch Publishing Limited
Printed in Great Britain by Oaklands Book Services Limited

Contents

Jane Degg, Over Whitacre, *c.* 1916. Jane was the younger of the two daughters of Thomas Degg of The Laurels, Over Whitacre. She is pictured here as a bridesmaid at a wedding of the Cornish family. During the First World War she ran away to Sheffield to marry Alfred Moss, a Smethwick man. Leaving her to return to The Laurels with her new-born son, Jack, Alfred signed up for the East Yorkshire Regiment. He was killed in action in France in 1918.

Introduction

This book includes photographs from the town of Coleshill and the surrounding parishes and settlements of Marston Green, Lea Marston, Maxstoke, Shustoke, Packington, Nether and Over Whitacre and Water Orton, the latter spilling over into Minworth for one or two important agricultural pictures. The western side of Coleshill is represented by a few photographs from Bacon's End, Tile Cross and Sheldon. Together they make up, as far as these things can ever be accurately defined, the traditional marketing hinterland of Coleshill. Even with over two hundred pictures, this selection can never hope to be wholly representative of these settlements, either individually or collectively. There have also been other volumes of pictures published for some of these places and we have, saving a few exceptional images, endeavoured to include only rarely seen photographs.

Coleshill and its surrounding villages have changed over recent years – something self-evident perhaps from the extent of new building activity in each community. However it helps to understand what the town and its villages were like in years gone by in order to fully appreciate just how much they have changed. That has to be one of the primary values of old photographs such as these; simply by looking at them you can glimpse what these places actually looked like, at various points in time, since photography became generally available. These pictures depict the detail of streets, houses and village greens in a way that the documentary sources of conventional history all too often fail to reveal.

Changes in the appearance of places can be easily be captured by the camera, but the camera can also capture something of the changing social character of each village and town. Populations seem to have increased as work opportunities in these rural communities have diminished. The rise of the commuter has gone hand in hand with the rise of motor vehicle traffic with all the ramifications that ensued. Coleshill is no longer the economic focus for the area, it is no longer even the dominant shopping area; Chelmsley Wood shopping centre and other 'out of town' supermarkets now hold sway. Village shops and post offices have also dwindled and disappeared. But more has gone than that. Town and village were each intrinsically bound by an inherent spirit of community that found daily focus around the workplace, school and shops, and is nowhere more poignantly revealed than in the scenes of town or village celebration shown in some of these photographs at, for example, the time of a coronation. Without television or video people's recreation time found expression in sports, plays, bands or other forms of social activity seen in the pictures that follow. How many of today's inhabitants shop locally or take part in any form of community activity?

Looking at the faces of our ancestors in these pictures we see pride, smiles and companionship, all of which can evoke a sense of nostalgia as we gaze at them. True, it was a quieter, slower way of life and stuck in the daily traffic jams at the Green Man cross-roads or Dunton Island, for example, it is easy to yearn for what appears to have been their gentler, less stressful existence. But although the 'camera does not lie', it can mislead. The photographer was never there to record the poverty, despair and ill health that inevitably at some time must have touched many of these people. To be awaiting news from husbands and sons away at war, facing the unemployment of the 1930s, or worrying about epidemics such as scarlet fever and whooping cough as they passed once more through local schools: there are no photographs to record these aspects of our forefathers' lives. The old brick and timber cottages seen here look quaint and inviting, but too many were also cold, draughty and horribly damp in winter.

We have tried to include accurate dates and captions for each of these photographs. Sometimes a precise date has been given, but in most cases the nearest decade is the best we can provide. Where caption space and memories allow, we have endeavoured to include the names of those depicted, but all too often a name still eludes us and we apologise to all those so omitted. The names of any row of people are always given from left to right. Where the name of the photographer or the source of the photograph is known, it has been added, in brackets, to the caption.

Acknowledgements

A great many people have kindly loaned us their precious family photographs to include in this book; some, sadly, are no longer with us, but we acknowledge them all none the less: Marjorie Atkins, Isabel Barnes, John Bellis, Margaret Bull, Sally Bragginton, Margaret Burchnall, Rita Callwood, Bob Carter, Norman Clayton, Sue Conway, Dolly Cooper, Mrs Court, Dorothy Cox, Jim and Iris Cox, Nora Crossland, Doreen Day, Sir William Dugdale, Dr Rosemary Edge, Annie Ensor, Bill Ensor, Rosemary Ensor, Bruce Gascoigne, Kathleen Gascoigne, Jack Green, Ruth Green, Mrs Griffiths, Joan Hancock, Bill Hartop, Mr Hastings, Peter and Jean Hayfield, Madge Hill, Elsie James, Ida James, Nan James, Kevin Jeromes, Margaret Johnson , May Keatley, Gordon Lane, Marjorie Lapworth, Jack and Mary Leeson, Eric Miller, Bill Moat, Miss Nevile, Nora Pickford, Beattie Robbins, Emily Rhodes, Howard Rumble, Jim Sampson, Hilda Simmonds, Lois Simmonds, Madge Smith, Nancy Stanley, Dr Jack Stuart, Mrs Tindall, Rex Tilson, Charlie Tranter, Joan Tuckley, Geoff Vaughan, Denis Walker, Edith Willis, Tom Wilson, Annie Wood, Joy Wright and Reg Wright.

We would like to thank the Birmingham Library Services for permission to use photographs from the Benjamin Stone Collection and the Warwickshire Photographic Survey. We would also like to thank Chris Foster of Warwickshire Public Libraries for permission to include photographs from their collection in Coleshill Library. We are grateful to Coleshill Town Council for the use of a picture from their archives, and to the Earl of Aylesford for the use of a picture taken in Packington Park. The *Birmingham Post and Mail* and Dubarry Studios Ltd have also generously allowed us to reproduce photographs under their copyright. John Miller and Alan Varley have very kindly given us permission to use their respective father's pictures. Most of all we would like to thank the people of Coleshill and the surrounding area for their generosity in searching through bureaux, attics and cupboards for their old photographs, and their help in identifying the faces and events depicted on them. We hope that this book will be a useful source of reference for the future, but most of all, we hope that it will prove both enjoyable to those who can still remember the times depicted and a fascination to those who wonder about the bygone world of their parents and grandparents.

John Bland and Colin Hayfield, *October 1996*

One

Farms, Farmers and Farming

Horse drawn reaper team, Coleshill area in the 1900s. Horse teams such as this had been working the fields around Coleshill for centuries, but within fifty years of this photograph being taken they had been almost completely replaced by tractors.

Dumble Farm, Maxstoke, c. 1906. Left to right are, a farm labourer, Mrs Ford, a house servant and Mr Frederick Ford the tenant farmer. Sitting in front are daughters Mynthia and Myra. Mr Ford was a working farmer, typical of the smaller farms in this part of North Warwickshire.

Degg family, The Laurels, Over Whitacre, 1896. (W.G. Chambers) Thomas Degg sits alongside his mother-in-law, Harriet Walker, and his wife, Catherine. Behind him stand his daughters, Jane and Harriet Elizabeth – 'Lizzy'. Thomas Degg was a typical small farmer, beginning his working life as a butcher and then, as he prospered, buying a small working farm here at The Laurels.

Threshing, Park Farm, Minworth, 1925. The gentleman in the dark cap on the left is Ernest Rumble, a gas engineer from Kynoch, who masterminded this attempt to run a threshing machine off a 110-volt electric motor using electricity reputedly supplied from the sewage works. It was not a success and the scheme was abandoned.

Foldyard, Dove House Farm, Shustoke, 1928 or 1929. Dove House Farm was then in the tenancy of John and Kathleen Alcock. The lad in the foreground filling the water buckets from the trough is unknown, but the one at the back loading the muck cart is thought to be Bill Phillips. In 1938 the Alcocks moved to Holliars Farm at Church End, Shustoke.

Kitchen chores, Bacon's End, Coleshill, 10 October 1942. Mrs 'Flossy' Mayne is in her kitchen at Charmaine on the Birmingham Road. Note the old Belfast sink and cold water tap.

Butter churning, Dove House Farm, Shustoke, 1927. Mrs Kathleen Alcock stands at the butter churn with young Kathleen Fox. The Fox family kept the Griffin Inn at Church End.

Above: Old Farm orchard, Hoggrills End, Nether Whitacre, 1929. The lady in black is Miss Lottie Hayfield who had taken over from her mother as the farmer here. She travelled weekly by train to Birmingham market with eggs, dressed chickens and small posies of local wildflowers. Sitting amidst the Light Sussex hens is her great-nephew, James Hayfield, whose father had the neighbouring farm, Hill Farm.

Right: Hill Farm farmyard, Hoggrills End, Nether Whitacre, 1914. Margaret Hayfield (later Johnson) is with her dog Tiger. She later became an infant teacher at Nether Whitacre School. On marrying she moved to Church Farm, Shustoke.

Blythe Farm rickyard, Blythe End, Shustoke, in the 1870s. On the left is George Wall, the tenant farmer here. The young man with the dog on the right is his son, James Bernard Wall, who was then a medical student.

Haymaking at Coleshill in the 1880s, taken in one of the fields that made up School Farm on what is now the area of Castle Drive and Wingfield Road, which Dr James B. Wall tenanted from the Digby Estate.

Henry Arms haymaking in Blythe Meadow, Coleshill, 1938. Henry Arms was a local jobbing builder who lived at No. 14 High Street. He rented his land in Blythe Meadow off the Grammar School Endowment Foundation, borrowing a horse from Willis's bakery whose premises lay along Blythe Road.

Annual horse show committee, Coleshill, in the late 1920s. This annual September event on the town cricket pitch was one of the highlights of the social calendar. A special viewing stand was erected and show jumping and other classes took place. The event died out with the Second World War. Left to right: Walter Bulpit (?), Arthur Lloyd, George Sale, -?-, -?-, E.P. King, Sidney Potter, Herbert King, George Willmott, Dr J.B. Wall, -?-, T. Wathes, -?-, William Morewood.

Darral's Butchers float, Lower High Street, Coleshill in the 1920s. Most villages had their own butchers who killed and cured their own animals. Harry Darral had a lock-up butchers shop on the Lower High Street, opposite the present telephone exchange building, although his main premises and slaughter house were in Water Orton beside the Digby pub. It is possible that the driver here was Sam Cooksey of Heathfield Cottages, Water Orton.

Smitton's Blacksmiths Shop, Coleshill, 1924. This blacksmith's shop lay up the side of the Coach Hotel. Left to right: Jack Smitton (blacksmith), Sid Cooper and Mr Moss. Joseph 'Sid' Cooper had been born at Ivy Cottage, Buckland End and had learnt smithying in the First World War. He joined Jack Smitton in 1924.

Mr Henry Field's Nursery staff, Coleshill, c. 1910. (Selwyn Ridge) At the top of Coleshill High Street and Parkfield Road, at the back of what is now the clinic, lay Mr Field's nursery, specialising in growing dahlias and other flowering plants for the local and Birmingham markets. Posed outside one of the greenhouses are, back row, left to right: Kimberley, Packwood, B. Rose, Henry Field, -?-, -?-, and front row: -?-, Clayton, Mrs Chatham, -?-, -?-.

Woodcutters, Coleshill Park, in the 1900s. (F.D. Spencer) In the medieval period the western part of Coleshill parish was still well wooded, but by the nineteenth century the only surviving large tracts of woodland were Chelmsley Wood, York's Wood and Alcott Wood . Odd trees survived in Coleshill Park and it is one of these that these men are believed to have been felling. The enormous size of the trunk suggests an oak of great age which must have represented a formidable task for these men, with only axes and large hand saws at their disposal.

Fencing work, Coleshill Road, Marston Green, July 1903. Estates, such as the Coleshill Estate, would have attempted to be self-sufficient in things like fencing. The steam engine here is driving a circular saw to cut and log-up felled trees into posts and rails. On the left are the trestles used for mortising the posts. The completed fencing can be seen stacked up on the left of the picture ready for use, indeed possibly to continue the field fence on the right which seems brand new. The horse and water cart in the centre of the picture would have been intended to provide water to keep the steam engine going.

Traction engine, Minworth, 1918. This traction engine formed part of the equipment of Tame and Rea District Drainage Board Farm, set up at Tyburn in 1878. By 1910 the Drainage Board farmed over 2,000 acres from Gravelly Hill to Kingsbury Mill, including land at Minworth Hall Farm, using sewage from the Birmingham area on the land. At the wheel is Bill Chilwell, while standing in front are Walter Collins and John Pittaway.

Steam ploughing, Minworth, 1918. Steam ploughing was a complex operation but proved useful on heavier soils. It involved two traction engines, at either end of the field, linked with chains or steel hawsers. The plough, attached to these chains, could then be winched backwards and forwards across the fields. As the plough could not be turned at the end of a furrow it had matching share and coulter on the other end that would be tipped over into use. Sitting at the plough is Harry Bourne, while Walter Collins helps set the equipment.

Reaping the corn, Bacon's End, c. 1940. Tractors began to be seen on local farms from the 1920s, but only began to effectively replace the horse in the late 1930s and 1940s.

Gordon Lane and threshing set, Lea Marston, in the 1960s. The Lanes were agricultural engineers, based here, adjacent to the old Boys School at Marston. The threshing set is being drawn by an old Field Marshall tractor.

Two

Transport and Industry

The carrier, Minworth Bridge, Water Orton, 1893. (Sir Benjamin Stone) Even after the arrival of the railways, horse drawn carriers such as this fetched and delivered goods across the county. Some were concerned only with local deliveries, while others travelled routes to a regular timetable across the region.

Postman Leeson, Forge Mills station, Coleshill, *c.* 1910. Forge Mills station opened in 1842, built on the newly opened line from Lawley Street, Birmingham to Whitacre. Joseph Atkinson was the station master here until the First World War, when Thomas Hartley took on the job. It was from this station that the town postman, Jim Leeson, dealt with the mail to and from Birmingham.

Original station buildings, Water Orton, in the early 1900s. (Sidwell, Meriden) This station was built in 1842 as part of the new line from Lawley Street in Birmingham through to Whitacre junction. The existing station buildings were erected in 1908 as part of an expansion of railway activity involving new lines, new sidings and considerably more trains.

Station staff, Whitacre Junction, c. 1910. (J. Rolfe, Small Heath) The old railway station had been built further north up the Derby line, opposite the Railway Inn at Whitacre Heath, but a new station was built here at the junction of that line with the new east-west line to Lawley Street. The station master was George Lambert.

Cycle tour visiting The Three Horse Shoes, Lower High Street, Coleshill in the 1900s. (Sidwell) The pub landlord at the time would have been Harry Shipley.

Cyclists, Coleshill in the 1900s. (F.D. Spencer) Sadly the names of the cyclists here are no longer known, but their dress is very smart. Cycling was still considered fashionable amongst the middle classes as very few could afford the new automobiles.

Right: Jim Leeson's motorbike, Hawkeswell Lane, Coleshill, in the 1920s. By the 1920s motorbikes were all the rage. Jim Leeson is seen here, fashionably dressed, astride his Triumph motorcycle. He was the youngest of six brothers and died in 1930 at the age of 47.

Below: New automobile, Hazelwood, Coleshill, in the 1910s. Sitting in the vehicle is B.E. Wall and his cousin, Eily Phipson. Bernard Wall was one of the first people in the Coleshill area to acquire a motor car and it was no doubt a strange (and noisy) sight to local townsfolk. But would they ever catch on? If only they knew!

Coleshill's first taxi, c. 1920. This Model T Ford taxi belonged to Tom Leeson who had established his garage in the High Street (now the site of the Coleshill Hotel) after the conclusion of the First World War. His brother, Jim, is pictured driving down Hawkeswell Lane to chauffeur Emily Walker to her wedding to Mr Rhodes. Rose Cottage can just be seen in the background.

Dabbs' lorry, High Street, Coleshill, in the 1920s. (Charles Crooke) From the nineteenth century Benjamin Dabbs had a brewery and bottling plant here, at the back of the old Three Tuns Inn, now the Golden Tandoori Restaurant. By the 1920s the operation was being run by Joseph Mosely. Beer was no longer brewed here, although Guinness was bought in and bottled. Instead, the bulk of the firm's business involved the manufacture, bottling and distribution of 'pop', particularly Dry Ginger Ale.

Phipps' Garage, Lower High Street, 1930s. During the early 1920s this building was owned by Sarah Prince, the garage being run by her son, Charlie, who drove a van for the parcel office and acted as a goods carrier from Forge Mills. The sign on the wall above the door says 'London Midland and Scottish Railway Parcel Receiving Office'.

Stonebridge Hotel, Packington, in the 1920s. This old inn expanded rapidly to take advantage of the increasing motor car traffic. In front of the mock half-timbered extension is a 'Filling Station', while to the left of the picture is what appears to be an early RAC telephone booth. Compare this picture with that on page 65 showing the same hotel some twenty years earlier in the pre-car era.

Flooding at Cole End, Coleshill, in the 1930s. Flooding was a relatively rare occurrence on the sort of scale shown here, but one very good reason why the new semi-detached houses, built along here in the late 1930s, were set several feet higher than the road surface.

Road mending gang, Coleshill, in the 1920s. (Selwyn Ridge) This Warwickshire County Council steam roller is being driven by Charles Keatley. A plaque on the steam roller records that John Wilmot was the county surveyor.

Accident, Coleshill High Street, c. 1950. (*Birmingham Gazette and Dispatch Ltd*) An army lorry collided with a double decker bus and overturned. There were about ten soldiers on the lorry, but nobody was severely injured. Traffic problems on 'the hill' had been alleviated by the opening of the town bypass, now the A446, in 1940, but accidents like this still occurred.

Accident, Coleshill High Street, c. 1950 (*Birmingham Gazette and Dispatch* Ltd) The same accident viewed from inside James' shop by Nan James and Ada Whitehead.

The reservoir builders, Nether Whitacre, possibly in the 1890s. Work had begun on building the Whitacre Waterworks in 1873. This team of men were presumably involved in the construction of the second, smaller reservoir built some years later.

Grimstock Hill Quarry, Coleshill, late 1920s. The proprietor of the Coleshill Sand and Gravel Company was a Mr R. Heseltine. Standing on the far left is Harry Hastings; the men are operating the Parker Plant for extracting the gravel.

Dabbs and Nicholson's Pop Shop, No. 107 High Street, Coleshill, *c.* 1935. Standing in their waterproof aprons are Nora Thompson, Sue Watkins, Freda Spencer and Florrie Hawkins. The two girls are Nora and Margaret Mosely. Here in the 'pop house' the syrup was made and the various colouring and flavouring essences added. Measured amounts were placed into bottles which were then filled with gas and water and capped. The apparatus was powered by an engine in the adjoining room.

Building Colehaven homes, Sumner Road, Coleshill, 1930. This elegant row of almshouses was built for the town by Sir John Sumner in 1930. The present Sumner Road was also created with the construction of these homes. Previously there had only been a pathway here between the High Street and Back Lane, which had been lined on either side with gardens and allotments. An additional four homes were added on the opposite side of the road in 1934.

Building Hams Hall 'A' Power Station, 17 January 1929. After the old Hams Hall house had been taken down, the 1,000 acre estate was purchased by the City of Birmingham and, in July 1927, work began on building the first section of the power station. Hams Hall 'A' Station was opened by the Duke and Duchess of York on 6 November 1929. This view shows the construction of the pumping station and reservoir.

Building Hams Hall 'B' Station in 1947. Work began on building the 'B' Station in the late 1930s, but it was not to be completed until 1949. Later, the 'C' Station was commenced in 1952 and finished in 1958. The chimneys and cooling towers dominated the landscape until their recent demolition in advance of the present construction of the new Hams Hall Inter-Modal Freight Terminal.

Three

Sports and Pastimes

Coleshill Social Club darts team, 1955/1956. Shortly after the Second World War the British Legion became Coleshill Social Club for ex-servicemen and moved into the vacant buildings of Orton College, just off the High Street. Left to right: Bert Pope, Vic Corner, John Rogers, Hilda Corner, Vic Cleever, Billy Kingham, Harry Barber, Peter Ratcliffe, Arkless Holland and Johnny Clayton. The team had won the Roland Cup.

Coach Hotel Bowling Club, Coleshill, *c.* 1900. Among those recognised on the back row are, Walter Farrin, Jack Clark, and Mr Somerfield (baker), and on the second row, Mr Blunt, Henry Leeson (watchmaker), Herbert King and Jim Leeson (postman).

Sons Of Rest Bowls, Coleshill, 1948-1950. Left to right: -?-, Bill Woodfield (bowling), John Dart, -?-, Charlie Lee, Walter Lee, -?-. The wooden clubhouse in the background was built by Charlie Lee and Mr Carter in about 1947.

Ladies' day, Coach Hotel, Coleshill in the 1920s. (Midlands Press Agency) Little is known of this event or of the people depicted, but the style of the ladies' dresses in particular suggests that it was regarded as a highly fashionable occasion.

Coleshill and District Bowls League winners, 1965. Back row, left to right: Bert Simmonds, Johnny Gough, George Baker, Bert Sampson, G. Matthews. Front row: Harry Cottrell (chairman), Billy Spencer (treasurer), Joe Darnell (captain), Billy Nicol (secretary), John Rogers. In front is the Debank Cup (winner G. Matthews), the District Jubilee Cup and the W.W. Green Cup (winner W. Nicol).

Junior cricket, Coleshill, 1926. Taken at the back of Cole End Farm, left to right: Dorothy Townshend, Jack Townsend, Evelyn Townsend, Dorothy Townsend (later Cox), Mary Townshend.

Coleshill Cricket Club, 1930s. (Selwyn Ridge) The four men in the front row are wearing the striped maroon and dark blue with gold pinstripes, club blazer. Back row, left to right: -?- umpire, Peter Tuckwell, Les Corbett, Jack Affleck, Bob Hextall, Bill Ensor, Arthur Leighton, Tom Ensor (groundsman). Front row: Frank Wrigley, Sid Chamberlain, Jack Nichols, Len Roe, Albert Ensor, Sid Treadwell. Scorer: Jim Boughton.

Nether Whitacre Cricket Club, 1946. Like many other local clubs, Nether Whitacre Cricket Club closed down during the duration of the Second World War and re-assembled on their old ground opposite the Swan at Whitacre Heath in 1946. Back row, left to right: Eric Crossland, John Pinfold, Maurice Barnett, Major Atkins, Arthur Luckett, Alan Luckett. Front row: Bill Luckett, Fred Houghton, Bill Gibbs and Chris Price.

Coleshill 'Imps' Cricket Team, 1930. (Selwyn Ridge) The Coleshill Young Conservative Cricket Team was part of the Imperial League, hence the name 'Imps'. The final took place in the Memorial Park and Coleshill won. The mixed-sex team comprised, back row, left to right: Ellen Jaques (nee Hazel), Les James, Wal Hazel, Ron Corbett, Eric Morris, Frank Chamberlain, Edith Antrobus (nee Jaques). Front row: Sybil Morris, Winnie Rigsby, Charlie Tranter (captain), Enid Treen and Thelma Weare.

Coleshill Football Team, 1910. The team and their supporters are posed on the banks of the River Cole just below Cole End Bridge. The larger silver cup on the second row is the Coleshill Charity Cup, provided about 1907 and competed for each Easter bank holiday Monday between the various local teams. In more recent years Dr Cant presented the cup, usually putting money in it to enable the winning team to buy themselves a celebration drink.

Comic football match, Coleshill, 1904. (F.D. Spencer) Joe Willis and Jim Leeson were part of a comic football match that took place in Coleshill that year with the proceeds being used for local hospitals.

Coleshill Rovers, 1934/1935. Back row, left to right: S. Hale, V. Griffin, J. Leeson, W. Smith, C. Dabbs, B. Brayshay, A. Smith, F. Clayton. Middle row, R. Tooly, B. Bull, A. Clayton, J. Measham, F. Southam, J. Sharard, J. Blyth. Front row: R. Williams, E. Southam, F. Kinser. The team were the winners of the Britton Cup.

Coleshill charity cup final, Coleshill, Monday 11 April 1955. (Harold Varley) The final in the Charity Cup, played as always on the Easter Monday, was between Coleshill Town and Dordon Athletic. Coleshill won by three goals to two. The Coleshill team comprised:
J. Cherry (goal), J. Brazier, D. Brazier (captain), A. Wilson, R. Houghton, B. Southam, G. Walters, J. Bradley, H. Stokes (centre forward who scored two goals), G. Brazier and N. Bradley (outside left, who scored the third goal).

Cuttle Meadow bridge, Coleshill, 1888. Young members of the Wall family play in the River Blythe watched from the bridge by their nurses.

Coleshill Scouts, 1920s. (C.W. Selby) The scouts are seen here floating a makeshift raft down the River Blythe between Blythe Hall and Blythe Bridge. Jack Simmonds was the scoutmaster at the time.

Cuttle Meadow bathing place, Coleshill, 1937. The bathing place lay just along the river bank to the north of Cuttle Bridge and the boys from the Grammar School used it as a regular part of their summer sports curriculum. This stretch of the River Blythe was very popular, particularly on warm summer days; indeed, it was here that most Coleshill children learned to swim. In the white cap to the left of the swan is Mary Phipps.

Woodland's Pool, Maxstoke, 1950s. The Woodland Health Camp was home to one of the first naturist clubs in Warwickshire and is still going strong. It was opened by Kath Burgess (now Hall) in 1938 in the twelve acres of Spring Wood at Maxstoke, hitherto part of Acorn Farm. This pool, built by members of the camp, was begun in 1939 and in use by 1942.

Coleshill Tennis Club, c.1935. Back row, left to right: George Barnes, -?- (holding racket), Gordon Neale, Maidie Barnes, Gwen Breedon, Staff Breeden, Emily 'Pem' Neale, -?-, -?-, Mrs Pridmore. Front row: John Barnes, -?- (on bike), Freda Pridmore (with dog).

North Atherstone Foxhounds, Coleshill, March 1936. The hunt walks forlornly down a snow-swept Coventry Road, passing Dr Wall's barn on the right. Mr Ansell was the master.

Four

Social Life

Bazaar Helpers, Nether Whitacre, c. 1905. (F.D. Spencer) Bazaars were occasionally held to raise money for church funds and were highlights of the village social calendar. Although many of these ladies names are now forgotten, those seated on the second row are, left to right: Mrs Charlotte Oldham (Croxall Farm), Mrs Rodgers (Oakfields), Mrs Mary Steel (School House), Mrs Metcalf (Rector's wife), Miss F M Barker (Halloughton Hall), Miss Gunning (Dingle Lane), Mrs Empson (The Dingle), -?-.

Wedding group, Church Farm, Shustoke, in the 1890s. (W.G. Chambers) This wedding involved the Haycock family, although details of the bride and groom are now lost. The tenant farmer, John Haycock, stands on the far right of the back row. Church Farm is one of the older farms in the area. The sandstone west wing shown here was built by Thomas and Katherine Croxall and bears a date stone of 1669.

Mr Jarman's wedding, Nether Whitacre, 15 May 1925. The Jarmans farmed at College Farm. Mr Jarman married a Miss Lawley.

Ethel's wedding, Coach Hotel, Coleshill, 1920s. (Selwyn Ridge). Standing, left to right: Wassie Fallan, Alice Milner, -?-, Jessie Milner, Ethel Milner (bride), -?-, -?-, Ann Bedford, Bill Daffern. Sitting in a chair on the right, cigarette in mouth, is Jack Lye (bridegroom), while on the far right are children Vincent Watson and, below him, Stan James.

Wedding of Rosemary Wall to Lance Edge, Coleshill, 8 September 1960. The popularity of the Wall family in Coleshill was reflected in the large crowd that gathered to watch this wedding. Rosemary Edge recalls that there were even people watching from up a lamp post! Although now retired, Dr Edge represented the third generation of Wall family doctors in Coleshill.

Above: Coronation procession, Lower High Street, Coleshill, 1911. (G.C. Crooke) The boys of St Edward's Homes lead the parade up the Lower High Street. Among the crowd on the left is the burly figure of Emma Scrivener, the landlady at the Green Man.

Opposite above: Coronation procession, Parkfield Road, Coleshill, 12 May 1937. (Eric Miller) Coleshill has always loved its processions up and down the High Street and it's not surprising that the coronation of George VI brought out the decorated floats and parades of local school children.

Opposite below: Coronation celebrations, Whitacre Heath, 1937. Nether Whitacre's celebrations usually took the form of celebration teas such as this one in the grounds of the old village hall, which is now a social club. As Nether Whitacre consists of several small hamlets and isolated farms, events like this brought the whole parish together.

Pearly king and queen carnival float, Coleshill, 1900s. (F.D. Spencer) Although the exact location of this photograph and the names of the people on it are unknown, it seems likely that this represents preparations for an early carnival parade.

Carnival parade, Lower High Street, Coleshill, 1924. This rather poor quality 'snap' illustrates not only an early carnival parade, but the background shows a rarely photographed part of the western side of the Lower High Street. Left to right: Phylis Clayton, Olive Watkins, Lottie Hastings, Edith Knight and Winnie Reader.

Parade band, Coleshill Carnival, 1950s. The band marches past the Cameo shop which stood in front of the cinema which had moved here in 1928. To the left of the picture can be seen the rear of one of Blackmore's coaches.

Water Orton carnival, August 1952. Carnival Queen, Rosemary Yeomans, rides in an open landau down New Road.

Dining room, Marston Green Homes, 1900s. (Nightingale) One feels sorry for these children having to pose so carefully for the camera in all their finery while each was no doubt keenly aware that their dinner was getting cold. Marston Green Cottage Homes were built by the Birmingham Board of Guardians in 1880 and are now occupied by the Brooklands Hospital.

Unionist's dinner, Coach Hotel, Coleshill, 8 March 1935. (T.F. Edkins) Among those dining in the Ann Bedford Suite are, on the front row: Harry Southam, Mrs Harris and Billy Harris. On the second row are Constance and Howard Court and Percy Walker, while on the back row can be seen Mrs Pridmore, Dr Cant and Frank Weare.

Afternoon tea, Coleshill, 1950s. Miss Edith Linforth and Miss Hilda Simmonds take afternoon tea together.

Musical chairs, Coleshill, 1959. (Holloway Studio, Birmingham) Children of workers at the ICI paint works at Station Road were treated to an annual Christmas party in the works canteen. In charge was the work's manager Mr Warwick.

Oddfellows' parade at the back of the Coach Hotel, Coleshill, 1890s. (A. Fletcher) The Oddfellows were one of the more popular of the self-help societies that flourished in the nineteenth century. The Coleshill Oddfellows used to meet at the Coach Hotel and each July they assembled on the Coach Green from where they marched to the church and held a service.

Coleshill Guides in the late 1920s. Guiding had started in Warwickshire with the formation of a group in Rugby in 1911. The 1st Coleshill Guides were formed in January 1923. Back row, left to right: Freda Pridmore, Beatrice Waller (captain), Harriet Stain, Mary Watkins, Barbara Allen, Kathleen Whitehouse, Ann Cant. Middle row: Annie West, -?-, Doris Wheeldon, Doris Miles, Ella Hazel, Sybil Morris, Barbara Whitehouse, Evelyn Townsend. Front row: Mary Barton, Grace Prince, -?-, Nancy Tranter, -?-, Margaret Pinney, -?-, -?-, -?-.

Water Orton band, 1900s. (F.D. Spencer) Little is known about this band but the fact that the band master is wearing a mortar board suggests that he may have been a local schoolmaster. The band consists of six cornets, one flugel horn, two tenor horns, two baritones, two euphoniums, two bases, three trombones and a base drum.

Coleshill band in the 1930s. (Lacy's Studios, Birmingham) Back row, left to right: Sid Clayton, Quintin Johnstone, Arthur Southam, Jim Gough, George Baker, Alf Wooley. Middle row: Jack Simmonds, Jim Sampson, Tom Neville, Len Simper, Archie Southam, Harry Southam, Ernie Southam, Bruce Gascoigne, Tom Mudd, Bert Simmonds, Cyril Clayton. Front row, left to right: Albert Clayton, Fred Clayton, Roy Mullis (musical director), Alfred Fifield (president), Norman Clayton (secretary), Bert Sampson. Seated, Charlie Woodfield, Arthur Senior.

Town hall fund bazaar, Coleshill, 1925. Fund-raising ladies from the Women's Institute are assembled on the vicarage lawn dressed in national costumes. A whole series of money-raising events was organised by various local societies and individuals within the town. The events included American Teas, jumble sales, dances, whist drives and a mile of one penny coins down the High Street. Some of the smaller children sold posies of flowers and there was even a competition to guess the weight of the vicar!

Opening of the town hall, Coleshill, 17 June 1926. Townsfolk and dignitaries are gathered for the opening ceremony which was performed by Sir Edward Iliffe MP, seen here in the centre foreground. On being presented with a silver key by the architect, Sidney Wigham, Sir Edward congratulated the people of Coleshill on the completion of the hall, saying that he was sure that it would become 'a centre where the social activities of the town would be drawn together'.

May Day celebrations, Over Whitacre, 1920s. For many years, while she was the teacher at Over Whitacre School, Miss May Oldham from Holt Hall Farm organised a May Day procession through the village. There was even a portable maypole for the children to dance around. Miss Oldham can be seen here standing next to the child holding the horse's head.

Opening of the British Legion, Coleshill, in the 1930s. (G.L. Bean, Water Orton) Mr Green, from Lansdowne House, Hoggrills End, was responsible for setting up the Coleshill branch of the Legion. They used this building opposite the Bell on the junction of Birmingham and Parkfield Road, formerly home to the Whitehouse family. Fred Dale was the caretaker. Many of the Coleshill Legion members joined the Home Guard in the 1940s.

Children's play, Institute Building, Church Hill, Coleshill, c. 1910. (C.G. Crooke) For many years the Institute was the base for Coleshill Operatic Society and also provided overflow classrooms for the Grammar School.

Woodlands' Amateur Dramatic Society, Coleshill, 1929 or 1930. These Methodist Sunday School girls are standing outside Mrs Pickering's bungalow, Woodlands, opposite the George and Dragon. Back row: Doris Simpson, Kath Walker, Freda Walky, Gladis Redding , Alice Simpson, -?-, Madge Farrin, Joyce Pickering, Jessie Sharrard, -?-, Emily Clark, Elsie Simpson, Mrs Pickering. Middle row: Elsie Warr, ? Stanley, Alice Miles, Nan Wright, ? Stilgoe, Rose Pennington , Valerie Burrows. Front row, Madge French, -?-, Marjorie Cooper, Mary Peach, Pearl Simpson, Doris Lavelle, Joan Lavelle. Sitting in front: Joan Adcock.

Women's Institute pageant, Warwick Castle, 1930. (Percy Simms, Chipping Norton) This picture was taken at one of the rehearsals of the Coleshill contingent at Blythe Cottage. They were representing the Ancient Britons. Front row, kneeling, left to right: Kathleen Nichols, Mrs Petrie, Heather Petrie, Mary Townshend.

Company of the Curtain, Village Hall, Water Orton, 1947. The play was Oscar Wilde's *The Importance of Being Earnest*. John Worthing was played by a Mr Vessey, Gwendolen Fairfax by Rosemary Yeomans, Cecily Cardew by Gillian Watson, Algernon Montcrieff by Gordon Pladel, Lady Bracknell by Miss Neale and Merriman the butler by Roy Hardwick.

Coleshill char-a-banc outing to Bath, *c.* 1910. (Edgar Wright, Bath) Once char-a-bancs such as this became more widely available they allowed a wide variety of day trip outings to be organised. Travelling at about 25 – 30 mph, this journey to Bath would still have been a long and arduous one.

Coleshill Darby and Joan Club outing, 1952. (A.H. Lealand, Coventry) Members of the Coleshill Darby and Joan Club on a cinema outing to Coventry.

Above: Young Conservatives, Coleshill, 1947. (E. Wadsworth, Water Orton) Back row: June Cole, Bill Hartop, June Ford, Evelyn Southam, Dennis Masters, Betty Brayshay, Stan James, Marjorie Prince, Bramley Saxon. Second row: Norman James, Mavis Fields, Barbara Prosser, Mary Evans, Audrey Prosser, Marion Davies, Joyce Brayshay, Jack Leeson, Chris McLaren. Front row: Arthur Pilley, John Hulm, Eileen Watton, Betty Watton, Shirley Clare, Joyce Draycott, Sheila Fields, Elsie Mayne, Janet Wright, Mary Leeson.

Right: Returning from Guide camp, Whitacre Junction, 1936. Back from their summer camp at Aber in North Wales are Nora and Madge Langford and, sitting, Edna Gibbs.

Coleshill Cinema, 1928. Coleshill's first cinema was situated alongside the Coach Hotel. In 1920 two recently demobbed navy men, Messrs Mason and Newport, opened this cinema in what had formerly been the brewhouse of the Coach Hotel. In 1924 George French, at the age of 17, took on the job as manager. The building seen here, fronting onto the High Street, contained the entrance hall, box office, projection room and toilets, while the cinema proper lay behind it. The cinema held about 200, with the seats set either side of a central aisle. Prices ranged from 2d at the front, to 9d at the back; right at the back there were also two curtained 'boxes' at 1/-, allegedly favoured by courting couples. The first film to be shown here was *Rags* staring Mary Pickford and took place as a matinee on a Thursday afternoon, which was then early closing day for the town. The films would arrive by bus from Birmingham and be returned the same way. Mr French is seen here standing in front of the cinema door and on the pavement to his left are the cases of film reels awaiting the bus back. The silent black and white films were shown with the aid of two old and rather temperamental projectors fed from an oil run generator in a small building outside. Mrs Townsend (nee Edwards) used to play the piano here, but with one film, *All Quiet on the Western Front*, a local lad, Eric Lee, was drafted in to provide mouth-organ passages. George French decided to bring in a small orchestral trio (piano, drums and violin), although this was later superseded by the use of amplified gramophone music, the operator having to skilfully switch from one record to another to suit the mood of the film. The cinema prospered and in 1930 it was moved to a new building known as the Cameo Cinema, a little further up the High Street.

Five

Pubs and Taverns

The Digby, Water Orton, 1900s. (F.D. Spencer) The landlord was T.J. Griffin. Good stabling was offered and parties were also catered for.

The Gate Inn, Nether Whitacre, 1910s. The landlady was Miss Elizabeth 'Bettsy' Ashmore.

The Tavern, Marston Green, 1930s. Coleshill folk could reach this pub by walking through Chelmsley Wood and it became a popular summer destination.

The Stonebridge Hotel, Packington, 1890s. (Sir Benjamin Stone) The Stonebridge Hotel was situated on the south side of what is now Stonebridge Island, and diagonally opposite the present Malt Shovel. Several ornamental garden trees that survive in the hedge line are now the only visible remains of this old pub.

The Dog Inn, Marsh Lane, Water Orton, 1930s. The pub has been photographed from the old iron girder footbridge across the railway. In the background, at the far end of Manor House Lane, can be seen several houses of the old village of Overton. These houses are now Hargrave House, Ferndale and Wakefield.

Friday auction sale, Green Man, Coleshill, c. 1910. (Whitehead's series) Coleshill had two weekly auctions, one at the back of the Swan and this one, held on Fridays, at the back of the Green Man. The auctioneer was Mr Bennet from Nuneaton. He would stand on a box under the lean-to-shelter, seen here to the right of the picture, and offer a variety of things for sale from furnishings and household items to sacks of potatoes and even small carts. Miss Hilda Simmonds recalled that one of the men who worked here was the town sexton, Charles Drakeford, and whenever there was to be a special sale of crockery he would walk down the High Street ringing a bell shouting 'crocks for sale tonight!' These auctions are thought to have stopped in the 1930s.

George and Dragon, Coleshill, 1900s. William 'Billy' Bissell was landlord of the George and Dragon from about 1900 to the First World War. He stands on the right of the picture, next to Mrs Ellen Walker, presiding over some form of celebratory meal. The many flowered buttonholes suggest that it could have been a wedding reception. This picture was taken in the old George and Dragon that fronted directly onto the Coventry Road. The pub was rebuilt in its present position in the 1930s.

Gardens, Coach HOTEL, Coleshill, 1920s. These gardens contained the bowling green and were also the focus for a whole range of social events. To the left is Bill James and next to him, Jessie James (née Milner); the elderly lady is Lydia Milner, while the lad on the bike is Stanley James.

Bar, Green Man, Coleshill, 1960s. To the left of the picture is Charlie Rowley while in the centre is Albert Lea.

Six

School Life

Playground, Shustoke School, Coronation Day, 1953. This was a little school at Church End situated at the end of the row of six almshouses that faced onto the church. They had all been built in 1699 by Thomas Huntbach. Miss Kate West (later Mrs Johnson) was the school mistress here for many years.

Coleshill Parochial School, 1870s. This picture shows the school as it was built by John Wingfield Digby in 1872, before its enlargement in 1890. It is now the town Civic Centre and home to the Coleshill Town Council.

Geisha girls, Coleshill Parochial School, 1900s. Sadly the names and event are now forgotten; is it a school play or revue perhaps? What an effort seems to have been put into costumes and parasols!

Coleshill infant school, 1950s. These temporary buildings were erected on the old school field, now Wheatley Grange, to serve as a nursery during the Second World War, but they later became used for infants. The teacher on the left is Miss Dorothy Heath, while that on the right is Mr Sid Chamberlain. Miss Heath became headmistress in 1940 and, until 1946, she was also Commandant of the Coleshill Company of the Girls Training Corps.

Coleshill Primary School class band, 1950s. Here is a scene that will surely evoke many a memory of junior school music lessons just like this. The range of music that could seemingly be adapted to drum, triangle, sticks and tambourine was a never ending source of amazement.

Coleshill Grammar School, 1907 or 1908. This is a French lesson in what is thought to be the old Grammar School on Church Hill about the turn of the century. The school was reputedly founded by Alice Digby in 1520, although it seems possible that a school of some form was already in existence by that time.

Coleshill Grammar School First Xi, 1918. (C.G. Crooke) Back row, left to right: Eric Besant, Eric Upton, Bob Waterson, Trevor Justin, Gordon Edwards. Sitting: Donald Edwards, Laurie Townsend, Herbert Thomas, Dick Line, Dick Hayfield. Scorer: Bob Gooderson.

Coleshill Grammar School, 1923. (Publicity booklet) The masters shown seated here were George 'Old Gilly' Gillyard, Revd Thomas 'Old Joe' Somerset Bateman, H.G. Stead and Percy C. Petrie. Somerset Bateman was one of several headmasters of Coleshill Grammar School who retired to be rector of Nether Whitacre.

Tom Wilson, Coleshill Comprehensive School, 1983. Tom Wilson, a former POW at Stalag Luft 3 (of the 'Wooden Horse' escape fame), took over the headship of the Grammar School from R.J. Green in 1956. He started the new school on the site at Coventry Road with about 227 pupils, but this rose dramatically to over 1,200 when the school became a comprehensive in 1971. He is seen here with secretary Betty Wells prior to his retirement in 1983.

St Paul's, Lower High Street, Coleshill, 1930s. (Moorwood's Series) Once an important house that, along with Cole End Farmhouse on the other side of the road, had stood sentinel at the foot of the High Street, St Paul's became the base for the Catholic homes until the St Edward's complex was established early in the twentieth century. It then became a Catholic school which, as the Central School, flourished during the inter-war years.

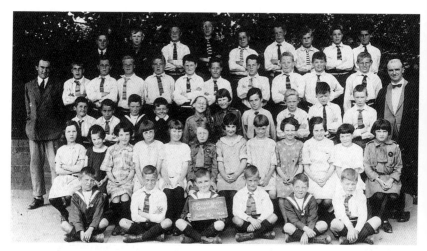

Central School class, Coleshill, 1926. Teacher Mr Wright stands on the left, and headmaster Vincent J. Curran, on the right. Among the pupils to be recognised are: Edgar Rose, Marie Miller (later Day), Nora Hawkins (later Thompson), Phylis Hawkins (later Hastings), Nora Moss and Mary Bryan (later West).

Orton College, High Street, Coleshill, c. 1945. Taken at the closure of the school are, back row:
Tom Bellwood, Jean Ingram, Janet Greig, Joyce Nichols, Elizabeth Dunning, Anne Cruise, -?-,
-?-, ? Rawlins, Rosemary Gold, Elizabeth Hall, Betty Blackmore, Joy Hancock, -?-, Glyn Hollis.
The teachers are Miss Annie Adcock, Miss Helena Adcock and Miss Noble. Kneeling: John
Blackmore, Patsy Curtis, Pat Walley, Gordon Beckerleg, Adrean Dunning, Dawn Bloomfield, -?-,
Janet Freer, Paul Matthews, Doug Bellwood, Sally Burton, Lorna Waghorn.

Maxstoke School, 1922. This was a public elementary school for about fifty children. Miss Frances
Hollyoak was the resident school mistress. Attendance at small rural schools such as this would
drop dramatically at harvest time when there was pocket money to be earned on local farms.

Lea Marston Girls' School, 1900s. Situated down School Lane in Lea village, the larger left-hand part of the building, seen here, was the school room, while the smaller part to the right was the school house. Although principally a girls school, it also took both boys and girls of infant age. Miss Mary Patstone was the school mistress and is probably one of the two ladies on the right of the picture.

Lea Marston Boys' School, 1907. Back row, left to right: Bill Lynes, Arthur Whitehead, Wilfred Bird, Walter Lane, Frank Stevenson, Bill Lewis and teacher James Redfern. Second row: Fred Jones, Albert Simmonds, Howard Bate, Mac Kinross, Bill Coton, Jack Bevan, Bert Coton, Tam Bevan. Front row: Eric Watson, Arthur Plummer, Herbert Thompson, Frank Fox, Ted Roberts, ? Lewis, Wilfred Watson, Arthur Smith. Kneeling: Harry Lynes, -?-, Howard Lane.

Marston Green Village School in the early 1920s. The teacher on the far right was a Miss Sarah Tart.

Nether Whitacre School, 1980s. (Simon Restorick) This photograph was taken shortly before the school was closed and shows head teacher Mrs Killips with her class. For generations village schools such as this forged an important and lasting bond between local children and their community and it is to the detriment of those communities that so many have now been closed as 'uneconomic'.

School room, Marston Green Homes, 1900s. (Nightingale) Marston Green Cottage Homes were built in 1880 on land in the south-west corner of Coleshill parish and were intended for pauper children in connection with the Birmingham workhouse. Eighteen cottages were built and, with the enlargements of 1911, they could hold 570 children. A church was added in 1905 and, in 1923, a swimming pool and an assembly hall.

Sewing room, Marston Green Homes, 1900s. (Nightingale) These homes were known for their strict regimes, but they also attempted to ensure that the children that passed into their care were trained in skills or crafts that would enable them to find employment when they left. Sewing classes were organised for girls, for example, and carpentry, boot-making or perhaps farming for boys. The site had its own 150-acre farm.

Seven

Church Life

Ringing the lunchtime bell, Coleshill, Friday 1 March 1935. (*Birmingham Gazette*) Sitting on the left is Geoff Bellis, while John Bellis rings the bell. Coleshill was more famous for its 8pm curfew bell; this lunchtime bell was rung largely for the convenience of shop staff. The ban on bell ringing during the Second World War broke both traditions and effectively brought about their end.

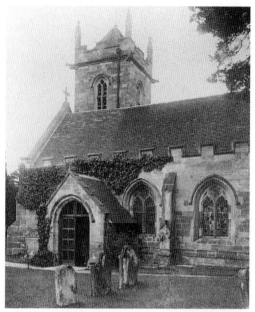

Left: St John's, Lea Marston, 1900s. (Sidwell, Meriden) The present church tower sits on the north-west side of the nave and is a later addition; early prints and paintings of the church show an original west end tower of traditional form. The church as a whole was heavily restored in 1876 and 1877 at a cost of £1,508.

Below: St Cuthbert's Rogation Day, Shustoke Green, Sunday 15 May 1955. The Rogation Day service sought blessings on the growing crops and would be held out in the fields and on village greens. This was a joint service between the Shustoke and Hockley choirs which was conducted by the vicar of Shustoke, the Revd W. Phillips.

Above: St Giles' churchyard, Nether Whitacre, 1900s. The elderly man sitting in the foreground was probably the sexton. Like other local churches, St Giles was also extensively restored in the Victorian period, this time in 1870.

Right: St Leonard's clock committee, Over Whitacre, 1949. The committee pose at the formal dedication of the new clock. Standing: Frank Knight, Mr Stitch, George Hammersley, Revd Stephen Knight, William Payne, Harry Grove. Seated: Marie Peebles, Mrs Gick and
Mary Conway.

Revd B. Jones-Bateman, 1900s. The Revd Jones Bateman (1825-1910) was rector of Sheldon for sixty-one years.

St Peter and St Paul, Water Orton. (F.D. Spencer) Originally a chapelry of Aston, Water Orton first became an ecclesiastical parish in 1871. The old chapel north of the railway in the old village was abandoned in favour of this new church which was built in 1879 at a cost of £3,940. The clock was added in 1921 as a memorial to those from the parish lost in the First World War.

Sunday school play, Church Hall, Water Orton, 1938. Left to right: Jessie Bevan, Sheila Yeomans, Eric Wadsworth, ? Brackstone, -?-(tall one), Ray Hawkins, Joan Shaw, -?-. Centre: -?-, -?-, Joyce Corbett. Front row: Wilfred Tabberer, Margaret Yeomans, Maurice Merriman, Peter Robertson, Vivian Bennett (turban), Harry Jenkins, -?-, Barbara Trethowan, -?-.

Above: Carol singers, Coleshill Church, Christmas 1958. (*Coleshill Chronicle*) The choir stands in the west doorway of the church with the Revd Frank Morgan.

Left: Congregational chapel, Birmingham Road, Coleshill, 1900s. Founded in 1834 and closed in 1972, this church served a small but dedicated congregation. Inset in the picture is a vignette of the local minister. His identity is uncertain, but he may have been the Revd Manoah Holland who was recorded as being the minister there in 1908.

Eight

War and Peace

Military recruiting march, Lower High Street, Coleshill, 1916. (Selwyn Ridge) With only carefully censored newspaper reports to inform people of the progress of the war, simple patriotism prompted many to fall in behind the colours on such recruiting marches, little aware of the realities of trench warfare that awaited them across the English Channel.

Simmonds family, Coleshill, 1914-1918. (Selwyn Ridge) Back row: Sam, Doris, Bill, Cissy and Arthur. Sitting: Sam Simmonds (senior), baby Georgie and Phoebe Simmonds. Sam Simmonds kept a greengrocers shop on Coleshill High Street next to the lych gate where Hawthorn's hardware shop now stands.

Explosive department, Water Orton Lane, Minworth, c. 1916. The assembled workforce of Frederick Mountford (Birmingham) Ltd stand outside their wooden hut factory situated at the back of the Drainage Board land, off the Water Orton Road.

In GRATEFUL MEMORY OF THE
SOLDIERS OF COLESHILL WHO HAVE LAID
DOWN THEIR LIVES FOR THEIR COUNTRY

Remembrance arch, Coleshill, 1918. Shortly after the end of the war this temporary evergreen decoration was erected around the Victorian wrought iron gateway into the churchyard. These gates, along with the rest of the churchyard railings, were cut down and sent for scrap as part of the 1940s war effort.

Recuperating soldiers, Maxstoke Castle, March 1917. Maxstoke Castle was one of a number of large houses that were used during the First World War to house the wounded. Nursing staff were largely drawn from the locality, few having much previous training.

Wounded soldiers, St Gerard's, Coleshill, 1916. (Selwyn Ridge) The new hospital unit, St Gerard's, that had been established on the Catholic homes site on Coventry Road, quickly found itself pressed into service as a military hospital for injured servicemen who had returned from the western front.

Victory celebrations, Church Hill, Coleshill, 1918. As ever, Church Hill was the focal point of the town's victory celebrations, photographed here from an upper room of the Swan Hotel.

Dedication of war memorial, Coleshill, 1921. Some years later Coleshill erected a lasting memorial to the fifty-five local men who died during the First World War. Standing to the left of the memorial is Archdeacon John Richards, vicar from 1920 to 1929. Next to him is Father Hudson; a uniformed group of his 'Homes Boys' can be seen in the centre foreground. On 17 March 1947 a great gale removed the ornate cross on top of the memorial; its replacement was a much simpler device.

Red Cross volunteers, St Gerard's, Coleshill, 1940. When the volunteers started at St Gerard's they were caring for babies and children evacuated from the Birmingham Children's Hospital. Dr Cant provided lectures on First Aid and Miss Kate Coaling, a retired hospital matron, provided lessons on home nursing. When the children returned to Birmingham many of these volunteers continued for a while at St Gerard's, helping with the orthopaedic patients.

American servicemen, Coleshill, 1940s. (Taylors of Handsworth) Although photographed in the Memorial Park, these men were billeted in Packington Park. During 1942 English soldiers of the Royal Ordnance Corps were billeted around the town to maintain and guard tanks that were stored along the newly created bypass (now the A446). They were fed in the Memorial Park in a purpose built wooden hut that later became the cricket pavilion.

Italian POWs, Maxstoke Castle, 1940s. Many of these POWs joined the labour force of local farms. Supervision rapidly became minimal as it became clear that most were only too happy to take part in the agricultural chores. In charge of the camp (now part of the golf course), was Major Atkins who remained in the area after the war and took an active part in Nether Whitacre Cricket Club (see page 39).

Coleshill Detachment Home Guard, 1940s. Sitting in the centre in the peaked cap is Captain Smith of Southfields Farm who was the officer in charge. On either side of him are junior officers Tommy Green and Percy Walker. Starting as the Local Defence Volunteers, many of these men were veterans of the First World War. Amongst their functions was the protection of the railway lines and Hams Hall Power Station.

Civil Defence Welfare Division in the early 1950s. (*Coventry Standard*) Cooking in the vicarage yard at Coleshill are, left to right: Mrs Knight, Annie Ensor, Mrs Shirley ? and Marjorie Jones.

Auxiliary fire tender, Coach Hotel, 1940s. The Auxiliary Fire Service occupied the range of buildings next to the Coach Hotel that had previously been home to the Coleshill Cinema (see page 62).

Meriden Rural District Council fire engine and crew, 1930s. (Selwyn Ridge) Back row, left to right: Jim Wheeler, Sid Cooper, Albert 'Toshy' Prike, Cyril Clayton, Harry Walker, Harry Phipps. Front row: Esmond Jacques (standing), Jack Baker, Fred Walker, Ernie Pickford (caretaker, Town Hall), Alf Hayward, Len Healey (driver and chief fire officer).

Special Constables in the late 1940s. (H.T. Chapman) Outside Coleshill Police Station are, standing, left to right: Arnold Cheetham (schoolmaster), Mr Tredwell, Harry Watkins, Ernest Willis, Ted Manton, Bob Hastings, Bernie Benson (gasworks), Ernest Pickford (caretaker Town Hall) and George Burrell (butcher). Seated: Arthur Willis, Bill Schofield (manager Co-op), -?-, and Charlie Plumb (Southfields Farm).

Dedication of new lych gate, St Peter's Walk, Coleshill, 11 May 1930. Councillors, members of the British Legion, scouts, guides, Oddfellows and choir had processed from the church down to the lych gate for the formal presentation from John (later Sir John) Sumner to the parish council. Left to right: Cllr Frank Weare (chairman), Cllr Alfred Fifield, Mrs Martha Sumner (nee Potter), Mr John Sumner, Revd W.R. Wyldbore-Smith, Cllr Jesse Reading, Cllr Fred Grew, Cllr William Linforth and Cllr George Ping.

Magistrates, Town Hall, Coleshill in the late 1920s. Among the magistrates present can be recognised Dr J.B. Wall and E.G. Hewitt. The side Council Room of the Town Hall became used for the local Petty Sessions.

Nine

Village Life

The old cross, Water Orton, 1893. (Sir Benjamin Stone) This old preaching cross was, by tradition, the focus for village worship before the construction of the original chapel here.

Children at play, Water Orton, 1893. (Sir Benjamin Stone) Note the disparity in the dress of the children: some, such as the lad on the far right seem expensively dressed, while other less fortunate boys, such as the one second left, had to make do with the coat and skirt of an elder sister.

Station Stores, Water Orton, 1900s. (Reeve, Water Orton) This range of shops on the Birmingham Road, opposite the station, was more extensive than an ordinary village might expect. It reflected the expansion of Water Orton in the second half of the nineteenth century, largely as a result of its railway station. The shop, just left of centre, was the village post office.

Birmingham Road, Water Orton, 1930s. This side of Water Orton developed after the building of the railway. To the right of the picture is the Methodist chapel.

The School and Green, Water Orton, 1937. (Golders Series) The school was opened in 1878. It had been built on the southern edge of the village along Attelboro' Lane facing onto an open space that became the village green.

Lord Norton, Hams Hall, Lea Marston in the 1900s. Charles Bowyer Adderley, seen here in the trap, was the first Baron Norton. Born in 1814, he was MP for North Staffordshire for thirty-seven years and a supporter of Disraeli. He and his family took a keen interest in local affairs, serving on local councils and as magistrates.

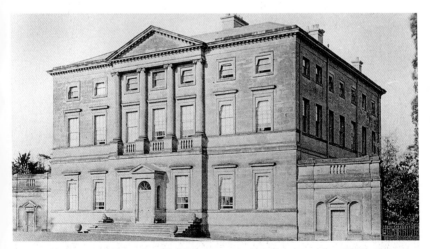

Hams Hall, Lea Marston in the 1900s. (F.D. Spencer) The hall was erected in 1760. Its interior was destroyed by fire in April 1890, although the library and pictures were saved. After the First World War Hams Hall was dismantled and re-erected at Coates, near Cirencester, Gloucestershire.

Village Green, Lea, 1895. (J.H. Pickard) In 1896 Herbert Edward Potter was recorded as keeping the post office and butchers shop in the building on the left of the picture. The post office was famous for its lion's head letter box. On the right, behind the parish pump, can be seen the buildings of Lea Farm. Both sets of buildings have since been demolished.

Village Green, Marston, 1895. (J.H.Pickard) Surprisingly little has changed from this scene of almost a hundred years ago; even the tree survives. The left hand part of the house on the left has been chopped off. What is now Holland Croft still stands on the right. Together, the two hamlets of Lea and Marston made up the parish of Lea Marston.

Boy's School, Lea Marston, in the 1900s. (Valentine's Series) The school was built in 1848 for ninety children and still stands just off what is now the main road from Dunton Island to Kingsbury. In the foreground is the school itself, while just behind it lies the school house, home at the time to the headmaster, James Redfern. At the time this picture was taken the school roll numbered about thirty-six.

Ivy Dean, School Lane, Lea Marston, 1900s. Ivy Dean was the home of the Nichols family, seen here in the foreground. Mr Nichols, on the right, was a carpenter at Hams Hall. The elder of his two girls, Amy, married Leslie Bate from Lea Ford Farm at the bottom of School Lane. The younger daughter was called Winnie. The house later became home to Henry and Annie Nurser and their daughter, Netta.

Walker family, The Firs, Hoggrills End in the 1890s. (W.G. Chambers) Mr and Mrs Walker stand with their four daughters, left to right: Annie, Nellie, Sarah and Polly. Mr Walker was one of the new breed of commuters, a professional man who lived in the village but earned his livelihood elsewhere. The Firs was reputedly built from the bricks of the original railway station at Whitacre Heath.

Coton Road, Whitacre Heath, c. 1910. To the left are a pair of cottages built in 1904: Temple on the left and Pathstruie on the right, while beyond them lies Coton House. Today they face onto the Buchan works. Coton was a small hamlet that lay on the borders of Nether Whitacre and Kingsbury, the site of which has now largely been lost by gravel working.

Family reunion, Hoggrills End, 15 May 1935. The inscription at the back of this photograph simply gives the date and says that it was at Hoggrills End. The location is thought to be the three cottages that went with the Oak Dean smallholding in Old Farm Lane. Frank Sharley, a Boer War veteran, lived in the centre cottage and it may be him standing with his wife on the far left of the picture.

Garage, Furnace End Cross-roads, Over Whitacre, 1930s. (Dubarry Studios, Birmingham) The garage had been started here in the 1930s by Harry Grove the butcher. He rented it out to Messrs King and Rice. Later, after the Second World War, Michael Titmus and Jack Moss took over, being in turn bought out in the 1950s by Alex Ingram

Above: Shustoke Green in the 1950s. There is a popular but mistaken belief that the settlement of Shustoke started around the church, now the hamlet of Church End, and moved down here to Shustoke Green after the Plague. In fact, settlements in many of the parishes around Coleshill have always lain dispersed into a range of small hamlets and clusters of farmsteads.

Left: Lucy Whitehead, Almshouses, Shustoke, 1960. (*Birmingham Post and Mail*). She stands outside her almshouse beside a giant 10 foot 3 inch high thistle. In his will of 1709, Thomas Huntbach had left provision for the construction of six almshouses for poor widows and others fallen into poverty. The bequest was supported by the yearly sum of £12 to be paid out of the rents of nearby Moathouse Farm.

Above: Pony and trap, Blythe Hall, August 1924. Driving the trap is Alfred Brooks of Cottage Farm and with him is Master William (now Sir William) Dugdale.

Right: Granny Guntrip, Blythe Hall, Shustoke, 1920s. Sarah Guntrip is seen here cleaning the doorstep of Blythe Hall, home, since the seventeenth century, to the Dugdale family.

Gatehouse, Maxstoke Priory, June 1888. (W. Jerome Harrison) The Augustinian Priory of Maxstoke was founded by Sir William de Clinton in 1336. This outer gatehouse is the most complete of the extensive earthworks and ruins of the priory. At the time this picture was taken Priory Farm was home to William and Ann Haddon.

Old Hall, Great Packington in the 1900s. (F.D. Spencer, Coleshill) The original timber framed hall was encased in brickwork in about 1679 by Sir Clement Fisher. King Charles was reputedly hidden here after the battle of Worcester in September 1651.

The Ford, Little Packington, 1900s. For generations the Ford was a popular local beauty spot although now it is all too often disfigured by litter and fly-tipping. The house and buildings in the background were once used as a school.

Royal house party, Packington Park, 1874. Princess Alexandra sits in the dog cart while the slightly portly figure of the Prince of Wales stands just to the left.

Gravel pit, Marston Green, 1900s. In the background is the church, while to its right is the post office. Marston Green in the 1900s was a small village that had developed on the boundary between Coleshill and Bickenhill. It was the arrival of the railway and the building of the Cottage Homes that started the rapid and extensive growth of the village to the point where it has now become virtually subsumed in the conurbation.

Village church, Marston Green, 1920s. Now demolished, this church was founded by the Revd J.D. Wingfield Digby some time before 1878. It was built of brick and designed to hold 180 people. With the building of the new church of St Leonards in 1939, this old building became used as the church rooms before being cleared to make way for housing.

Post office, Marston Green, 1900s. Situated opposite the church, this post office doubled as a tea room and shop. At the turn of the twentieth century Miss Mary Linforth was sub-postmistress here.

Marston Green, 1930s. This traffic island still stands at the junction of Station Road with Alcott Lane. Just discernible in the centre of the picture is The Tavern (see page 64), now rebuilt as The Marston Green Tavern. The petrol pumps on the right mark what is now the Marston Green Service Centre, while the house beyond it is currently the post office.

Above: Laburnum Cottage, Tile Cross, 1900s. Now demolished, this cottage lay on the west side of Cook's Lane, just down from Bacon's End cross-roads, opposite what is now the City Technology College at Fordbridge.

Left: Granny Jenkins, Tile Cross, 1900s. Born at Malt House Farm, Tile Cross, Martha Jenkins is seen here sitting outside Laburnum Cottage.

Opposite above: Sheldon Hall, 1900s. At the time Sheldon Hall formed part of the Coleshill estate of the Digbys and was tenanted to George and Eddie Kitchen.

Opposite below: Babb's Mill, 1920s. This three wheeled undershot mill derived its name from a former owner John Babb, who died in 1651. It later became part of the Digby's Coleshill estate until its sale in 1919 when the associated cottage was described as containing 'parlour, kitchen, scullery, and three bedrooms'. In the foreground is Bill Bloxham, a jobbing builder, who operated from a small yard here behind the mill.

232-11 Cross Roads, Bacon's End, Chester Road.

Bacon's End Cross-roads, 1920s. This view is taken looking along the Chester Road from Castle Bromwich; the signpost shows Coleshill to the left and Cooks Lane to the right. Today this busy junction is dominated by a traffic island and filling station.

Charlie Prince's Post Office van, 1920s. Based at what was later known as Phipps' Garage along the Lower High Street (see page 29), Charlie Prince operated a post office parcel office, delivering parcels in this van around the Coleshill area.

Ten

Town Life

Coleshill from the north-west in the 1920s. This view was taken in the years before the town bypass road, now the A446, cut a path across the western side of the town fields. In the centre left of the picture the light coloured walls of Cole End Mill can still be seen.

Lichfield Road, Cole End, 1920s. (Whitehead's series) Here Lichfield Road is seen looking westwards from the Wheatsheaf, with one of the bay windows of the Queen's Head pub visible to the right of the picture. The Queen's Head was one of the last coaching inns to be built in Coleshill in the early part of the nineteenth century but never seemed to prosper. By the time this photograph was taken it had been divided into a number of houses.

Baldwin's Electrics, Lichfield Road, in the late 1920s. The shop signs advertise that they were 'electrical and wireless engineers' and that 'Accumulators [were] charged and supplied'. Mr Baldwin installed electric wiring in Mrs Barton's house, the Newlands, Coventry Road, the first house to be wired for mains service in the Meriden area. As a result of his many local installations, Coleshill was the first town to get a mains supply from the Birmingham Electric Supply Department's Nechells power station.

Above: Lower High Street, 1950s. Hidden behind these houses were a number of yards, each with several houses along them. At the back of the Three Horse Shoes, for example, was Shoes Yard containing three houses and Wisteria Cottage. To the left of the picture is the administrative block for St Paul's School, and next to it, at No. 3, Mrs Roberts is seen calling at the door of Tommy Meeham the school caretaker.

Right: Smith family, Lower High Street, in the late 1930s. On the left is Fanny Maria Townsend, on the right, Harriet Smith, while in front is Richard Smith. The picture was taken outside one of the four back-to-back cottages at No. 31 High Street. The Townsends and the Smiths lived in the front two, and Mrs Wright and Mrs Harriet Smith in the back two. There were pigs and ash pits (miskins) at the rear of the properties. Each cottage was rented at 6/- a week from a Mr Wolstram.

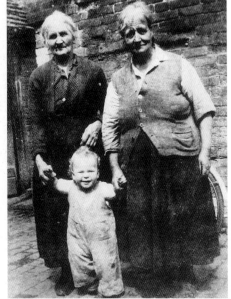

Co-op van, Lower High Street, 1920s. Standing by the horse is Walter Heywood who drove the delivery van for the Co-op. Both horse and cart were kept at the back of the Swan Hotel, the bread being delivered daily from a bakery at Stechford. Coleshill was Branch No. 1 of the Birmingham Co-op.

Jubilee celebrations at Tilley's Shop, Lower High Street, 12 May 1935. Left to right: -?-, Mary Linforth, -?-, Mr Tilley and Mrs Tilley. One of the newspaper posters' headlines records the Wimbledon tennis player Betty Nuttal.

Lower High Street, 1957. (Harold Varley) Here the Lower High Street is seen from just below the cross-roads. To the left of the picture is Mr Wear's grocery shop, then the homes of the Jerromes and the Knights. Further down amongst the low range of buildings in the centre of the picture is Sturmey's saddlers, while beyond that is Linforth's shop.

Blythe Road in the late 1950s. (Harold Varley) The road is viewed from the Green Man cross-roads, on the left is the corner of James's shop and, on the right, Child's fish shop. Behind the low range of buildings up on the left used to stand the Coleshill workhouse. Just over the hill on the left was the old Turk's Head Inn while behind it lay Willis' bakery. Approaching the cross-roads is a Vauxhall Victor Mark 1.

The Hill, 1930s. In the background is Hams Hall 'A' Station, where work had begun in 1926 and was completed in 1929; the later 'B' Station was commissioned in 1942. The 'A' Station was constructed in the southern part of Lea Marston parish on the site of Hams Hall, the ancestral home of the Adderley family.

Vintage car, The Hill, 1950s. (Eric Miller)

Church Hill in the late 1930s. (Moorwood's Series) On the left, the town pillory stands outside the Institute Building. Moving up the hill there is Deveraux House, home of Mr Fred Pinney, who was the Digby's agent for their Coleshill estate. Beyond that is the Old Bank House, later used for a while as Council Offices. At the top of the hill is the old Grammar School where Ronald Green would have been headmaster when this picture was taken.

Swan Hotel, 30 March 1929. (E. Miller) This is one of Eric Miller's first pictures of Coleshill. His father, James Miller, had the double fronted drapers and agricultural outfitters shop between Crooke's chemists shop and the Swan Hotel. He joined his father in running the shop in 1936, staying until his retirement in 1971. Along with Harold Varley, Eric Miller took a remarkable series of photographs of Coleshill during the great phases of demolition and rebuilding in the 1960s and 1970s.

Above: Varley's Chemists, 1950s. Harold Varley had taken over Spencer's old chemists shop from Charles Crooke, while the shop next door, formerly Albert Blunt's watchmakers premises, was used by Gwen Breedon as a florists before she moved up to Tudor House.

Left: Cosy Café, 1920s. This small café lay at the back of Taylor's bakery and was accessed from what is now St Peter's Walk.

Opposite: Mallaber's Butchers, 1930s. Mallaber took over the butchers shop from Drakefords and held it for a number of years before Hulls took over.

Dr Wall, Hazelwood, High Street in 1880. James Bernard Wall spent his childhood at Blythe Farm, Shustoke and, after qualifying as a doctor, took up practice in Coleshill. He was a keen horseman and managed to breed horses and maintain his interests in farming by renting School Farm from the Digby Estate. He was a long standing supporter of the annual Coleshill Horse Show (see page 16).

Hazelwood, High Street, 1888. Viewed from the rear of the property, a nurse is holding baby Bernard Wall.

The Wall children, Hazelwood, 1894. The children are, left to right: in the pram, Francis Geoffrey Wall and Kathleen Wall, in the deckchair, Bernard Wall.

The Wall children, 1894. Young Bernard Wall pulls his sister Kathleen, while in front sits their grandfather

High Street, 1890s. On the right is Waltham House, later home of Dr Cant and now known as Queen Ann House. The tree on the left stands in the gardens of Ivy Lodge, later Orton College, now Coleshill Social Club.

Coleshill town hall, 1926. (C.G. Crooke) The land for the new public hall was found from two adjoining plots; one was part of the glebe called Paston's Croft which was donated by the vicar, while the second was provided by Major F.J.B. Wingfield Digby. By July 1925 over £2,000 had already been raised through fund-raising and the contract was signed to commence the building. The architect was Sidney Wigham of Ward End, Birmingham, and Harry Dare was the builder.

Upper High Street, 1900s. (Whitehead's Series, Coleshill) This view is taken looking north, with Maxstoke Lane off to the right. Beyond that on the right is Fern House, home of Hartley Dabbs, then Coleshill Cottage, home to the Dale family seen below and after that Coleshill House, now the library and local residence of the Wingfield Digbys.

The Dale family, 1890s. Mr and Mrs Dale sit with their four children; the girls are Lily and May.

Father Hudson's Catholic Homes, Coleshill, 1950s. Development here began with St Edward's, which opened on 6 November 1906, followed by St Gerard's Hospital in May 1913. The school and chapel opened in 1915, the central office and Cottage Homes in August 1925 and St Joan's in about 1930. It was all part of the Birmingham Diocesan Rescue Society set up by Bishop Ilsley in 1902 with Father Hudson as secretary.

Grass cutting, St Gerard's, 1920s. Ivor Bolies holds the handles of the horse drawn lawn mower, while at the horse's head stands William Simpson who was head gardener at Father Hudson's Homes from 1905 to 1969.

Christmas at St Gerard's, 1950s. Christmas is celebrated in one of the 'outdoor' wards, Ward 8. Sister Brendan, who presided over the ward for thirty years, is visible on the left (Brendan Close was subsequently named after her). In the background is the large Nativity scene which came out year after year. There are still nuns at St Gerard's, but they no longer wear the traditional heavy habit of former days.

Dr Stuart at St Gerard's, 1950s. The Christmas Day ward round takes place at St Gerard's. Note how close the cots were to each other. Children often stayed in these wards for months or even years with TB or polio. Dr Stuart, seen here, shared in looking after St Gerard's from 1949 to 1989. With him is one of Dr Wall's daughters, Helen. Dr Wall had looked after St Gerard's from its foundation in 1918 until Dr Stuart joined him in 1949.

Coventry Road, *c.* 1900. The flags are out, but the reason is unknown. The date of the photograph might suggest either Queen Victoria's Jubilee, or perhaps the coronation of Edward VII. Mr Peach's house, seen on the photograph below, is on the left hand side of the picture.

Peach's Hairdressers, *c.* 1933. Local hairdresser, Harry Peach, stands outside his house at No. 22 Coventry Road. He was apprenticed as a hairdresser at Droitwich and then moved to Stratford before taking on the business at Coleshill. This cottage was one of a pair, that to the right of the picture belonging to Mr Field whose nurseries lay at the back of these cottages.